P9-DMA-412

ER 796.068 BLO
Bloom, Paul, author.
Rules on the playground

The School Rules

RULES ON THE PLAYGROUND

FOUNTAINDALE PUBLIC LIBRARY DISTRICT
300 West Briarcliff Road
Bolingbrook, IL 60440-2894
(630) 759-2102

By Paul Bloom

Gareth Stevens
PUBLISHING

Please visit our website, www.garethstevens.com. For a free color catalog of all our high-quality books, call toll free 1-800-542-2595 or fax 1-877-542-2596.

Cataloging-in-Publication Data

Bloom, Paul.
Rules on the playground / by Paul Bloom.
p. cm. — (The school rules)
Includes index.
ISBN 978-1-4824-2657-1 (pbk.)
ISBN 978-1-4824-2658-8 (6 pack)
ISBN 978-1-4824-2659-5 (library binding)
1. Playgrounds — Safety measures — Juvenile literature. 2. Schools — Juvenile literature. 3. Etiquette for children and teenagers — Juvenile literature. I. Bloom, Paul, 1963-. II. Title.
GV424.B56 2016
796.06'8—d23

First Edition

Published in 2016 by
Gareth Stevens Publishing
111 East 14th Street, Suite 349
New York, NY 10003

Copyright © 2016 Gareth Stevens Publishing

Editor: Ryan Nagelhout
Designer: Laura Bowen

Photo credits: Cover, p. 1 Deborah Jaffe/Stockbyte/Getty Images; pp. 5, 24 (playground) alex2004/ Shutterstock.com; p. 7 © iStockphoto.com/damircudic; p. 9 Samuel Borges Photography/Shutterstock.com; p. 11 Pressmaster/ Shutterstock.com; pp. 13, 24 (swing) wong sze yuen/Shutterstock.com; p. 15 Sergey Novikov/ Shutterstock.com; p. 17 karelnoppe/Shutterstock.com; p. 19 Len44ik/Shutterstock.com; pp. 21, 23 2xSamara. com/Shutterstock.com.

All rights reserved. No part of this book may be reproduced in any form without permission in writing from the publisher, except by a reviewer.

Printed in the United States of America

CPSIA compliance information: Batch #CS15GS: For further information contact Gareth Stevens, New York, New York at 1-800-542-2595.

Contents

My friends love
the playground.

We go play there
after class.

Every playground
has rules.

Rules help
keep you safe.

Take turns
on the swings.

Play nicely with others.

My friends like
to play tag.

Let others use your toys.

I bring a ball
to the playground.

We use it to play catch.

Words to Know

playground

swing

Index